REAL TEXANS
DON'T DRINK SCOTCH
IN THEIR DR PEPPER

Bill Walraven has been a daily
columnist for the *Corpus Christi Caller*
for 15 years.

Jerry LaPorte is an artist and partner in
the Corpus Christi advertising firm of
Morehead, Dotts, LaPorte, and Gilmartin.

Portions of this book were originally published in the
Corpus Christi (Texas) *Caller*.

Printed in U.S.A.

HOW IT HAPPENED

The idea for *Real Texans* was born at Scholz's Beer Garten in Austin.

Someone mentioned quiche. Someone else brought up Real Men, and someone interrupted, saying, "A Real Texan would put jalapeños in his quiche."

That started a game that continued for weeks. It became a traveling game between the author and his wife. The results were laundered into newspaper columns, extended by suggestions from readers.

The author purposely avoided naming examples of Real Texans (or Unreal Texans) because he is allergic to teeth bouncing off the floor. Every now and then a fancied Real Texan becomes angry at the mention of one of his foibles, i.e., a Toyota pickup or catsup on his hamburger.

Actually, this nonsense is directed to all Texans: real, drugstore, newly arrived or accidental. No insults intended. Real Texans tend to be heavily armed.

REAL TEXANS DON'T DRINK SCOTCH IN THEIR DR PEPPER

By Bill Walraven

Illustrated by Jerry LaPorte

Published by Sandcrab Press
P. O. Box No. 1479
Corpus Christi, Texas 78403

First printing, September, 1982 by Commercial Printing Co., Corpus Christi, Texas

ISBN 0 9609 870-0-2

INTRODUCTION

There have been books written about Real Men and Real Women. Why not Real Texans?

Real Texans are Real Men and Real Women and a whole lot more. A Real Texan may be extracted from Mexican, German, Czech, Pole, Irish, Black, or Anglo American, or others. He may prefer tortillas, koch kasse, or cornbread and turnip greens.

The Real Texan has become stereotyped as a Texas windbag. A Real Texan is not a braggart. He knows he doesn't have to brag about Texas. He is known to walk and talk slowly. That is because of the Texas heat. You don't do anything very fast when it's that hot. The slow walk comes from all parts of Texas. Out in West Texas it's the sand that slows it down. In East Texas it's the mud. In South Texas it's the thorns, cacti and sticker burrs. In the Panhandle he walks cautiously to keep from slipping on the ice and snow or being blown down by north winds.

Historians have varied views of the Texan. T.R. Fehrenbach described historic Texans as those who could die valiantly at the Alamo but who took orders with poor grace.

D.W. Meining said the Texan is strong, individualistic, egalitarian, optimistic and provincial. He accepts violence as an appropriate solution to certain problems . . . feels superior to others and is suspicious of outsiders.

Author Berl Pettus says Texas is "incessantly in love with its myths, and images of gushers, Cadillacs and invincible football teams."

J. Frank Dobie said of early Texans: "They did not lie, cheat, oppress the weak, discuss respectable women, or backbite."

Historian Joe B. Frantz said the Texas man "is expected to be tall, skinny, friendly, quick-tempered, charitable toward his friends and

7

merciless toward his enemies, shy around good women, a hell-horse with more compliant ones, and a possessor of a dozen other recognizable stereotypical attributes."

They are all right and all a little wrong. This book is designed to bring you up to date on what the modern Real Texan is about, sort of.

The author does not claim to be a Real Texan, though he is native-born. To start with, a Real Texan would never major in journalism (apologies to Walter Cronkite, Bill Moyers and Dan Rather). If a Real Texan did major in journalism, he would become a public relations man for an oil company as a steppingstone to the Texas Legislature, where he would lose all right to being a Real Texan. But he would be rich enough to dress and act like a Real Texan.

The author confesses he does not own a pair of cowboy boots, a pickup truck, a ranch, or a hunting lease. His one cowboy hat, abandoned by someone on a trail ride, is so disreputable a sheepherder wouldn't wear it. But the author, as a dispassionate observer, has lived among Real Texans all his life. Some of these observations appeared in the *Corpus Christi Caller*. Many were supplied by readers.

The author is grateful for their assistance.

A Real Texan wouldn't write a book like this, but he would read it to see if he really is one.

—Bill Walraven

CONTENTS

DRINKS

Real Texans don't drink Scotch in their Dr Pepper.

A Real Texan doesn't drink Perrier Water, ever. He drinks branch water properly sterilized with a good grade of sour mash whiskey.

A Real Texan knows a longneck is not a Whooping Crane.

Real Texans prefer Shiner beer to pot or pills.

It's a Real Texas wedding when they serve Pearl instead of champagne.

A Real Texan might strangle if he drank beer out of a glass.

A Real Texan can throw off two ounces of tequila with salt and lime without throwing up or turning purple.

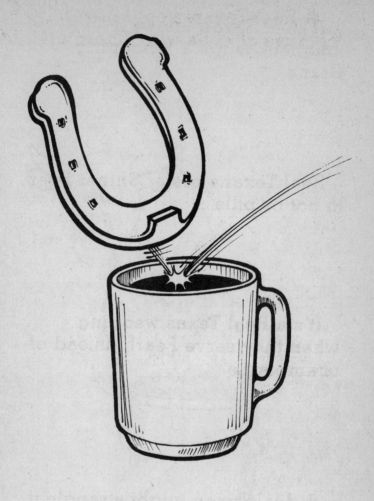

A Real Texan knows the coffee isn't done if a horseshoe won't float in it.

A Real Texan never washes out his coffee cup. That destroys the flavor.

A Real Texan would never confuse chablis with Charolais.

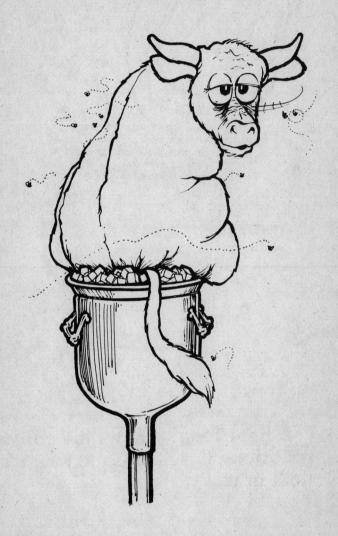

Most Real Texans won't drink Scotch at all. They'd just as soon drink their Dr Pepper straight.

EATS

A Real Texan will eat quiche only if it is well-doused with jalapeño peppers and eggs only as huevos rancheros, with the hot stuff built-in.

You know he isn't a Real Texan if he cuts his taco with a fork. A Real Texan uses his fingers to eat fried chicken, french fries, and burritos, and sometimes he uses his foot if whatever is on his plate is still moving.

Real Texans don't accept food stamps. They'd eat 'possum first.

A Real Texan doesn't eat raccoons, armadillos, or jackrabbits. But in case the Depression comes back, he knows where to find them.

To a Real Texan, barbecued pork is not Kosher.

Real Texans think 36-inch pipelines were invented so they could make barbecue pits out of them.

A Real Texan would not consider barbecueing with hickory if mesquite was within driving distance.

A Real Texan knows you can sell a second-rate steak if you put it on a sizzling platter.

A Real Texan orders a double double all the way at the hamburger stand.

Real Texans know that yogurt is plain old thick clabber.

Real Texans think pot is something that goes before likker — to eat over cornbread.

A Real Texan prefers cornbread over light bread. Also he doesn't like having to pay extra for 3.2 beer, 80 proof whiskey, six percent wine, cigarettes with no tobacco in them, and gasoline with the lead out.

Real Texans DO remember to
take the shucks off tamales
before they eat them.

Real Texans do not eat lunch.
They eat dinner. For Sunday
dinner they eat fried chicken.

A Real Texan does not eat in a
restaurant. He eats in a cafe.

CHILI

Real Texans can make chili
without Wick Fowler.

Real Texans do not ruin
perfectly good chili with
hamburger meat, beans, or
macaroni.

Real Texans do not put brown
sugar in their pinto beans. You
don't cook candy and frijoles in
the same pot.

A Real Texan knows it's damn good chili if it makes his ears ring, his nose run, and sweat drip from his brow.

A Real Texan will not eat jalapeño lollipops, jalapeño sherbet or jellybeans — insidious Yankee plots to undermine the Republic.

WHEELS

A Real Texan believes in law and order, except when the law has radar.

A Real Texan will walk or hitchhike before he will ride a bus.

A Real Texan believes the traffic jam is a Yankee invention. That's why he does not lean on his horn in traffic.

Real Texans always observe
the 55-mile-an-hour speed limit
— on parking lots.

A Real Texan thinks yellow
traffic lights are really a pale
shade of green.

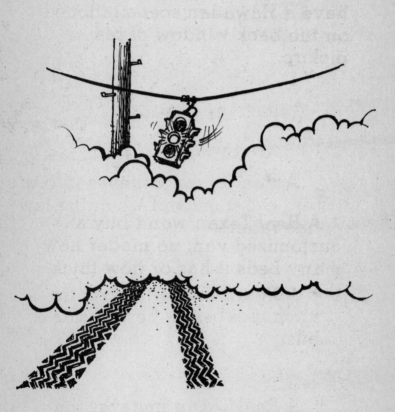

A Real Texan considers it pretentious to have his Cadillac washed and waxed.

A Real Texan would never have a Hawaiian scene tattooed on the back window of his pickup.

A Real Texan won't buy a customized van, no matter how many beds it has or how thick the rugs.

To a Real Texan the bumper sticker, "THE UNIVERSITY," is Austin-tatious.

A Real Texan never honks his horn in a traffic jam. He's never seen a traffic jam except the one time he went to Houston.

A Real Texan doesn't order four-wheel drive unless he needs it to get across his yard.

A Real Texan never washes his pickup. The dirt helps the rust hold it together.

A Real Texan uses the dashboard of his pickup as a filing cabinet for his important papers.

Real Texans don't build their pickups 10 feet high with bulldozer tires.

Real Texans keep a chiropractor on retainer. They have to, with their pickup rifle racks right behind their necks.

Real Texans don't lock their pickup toolboxes. Tools are perfectly safe with a 150-pound dog back there.

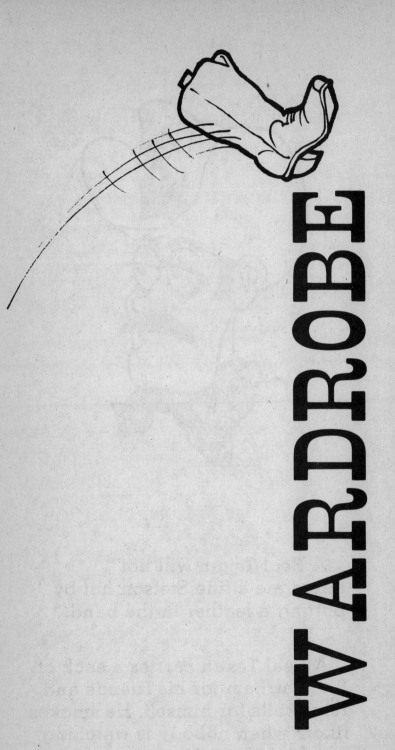

WARDROBE

A Real Texan will not
desecrate a fine Stetson hat by
putting a feather in the band.

A Real Texan carries a sack of
Bull Durham for his friends and
readyrolls for himself. He smokes
filters when nobody is watching.

A Real Texan will not wear a snakeskin hatband unless he kills the snake himself and tans it out.

A Real Texan doesn't need sunglasses. He just squints.

Real Texans wear designer jeans by Wrangler.

A Real Texan doesn't wear a ring in his nose. He wears it on the seat of his britches where a Garrett snuff tin wears on the hip pocket.

Real Texans with high-pitched voices wear jeans that are a shade too tight. There is no such thing as too-tight jeans on Real Texas Women.

The big belt buckles Real Texans wear aren't chastity belts. They just work out that way sometimes.

A Real Texan never wears socks with his shorts unless he's wearing his boots.

A Real Texan carries a red mechanic's rag in his hip pocket until he goes formal. Then he changes to a bandana.

A Real Texan does not resent it when asked how his boots got dirty.

A Real Texan will never complain his boots are too tight, unless his wife bought them.

Real Texans don't buy boots with walking heels. If God had intended for man to walk, He wouldn't have made horses.

OUTDOORS

A Real Texan does not own a Japanese pickup, a wet bike, or a wetboat.

A Real Texan loves nature and all its creatures. He loves to shoot deer, javelinas, rabbits, quail, turkey, and varmints.

Real Texans don't sit there and wait for fish to come to them. They wade out in the water and get them. And they don't hunt from a heated blind. They stalk their game.

A Real Texan will never go for a .22 caliber varmint gun. He likes a .44 magnum over rat shot.

A Real Texan keeps a
taxidermist on retainer.

A Real Texan puts huge
spotlights on his pickup so he
can scare deer away from camp
at night.

A Real Texan will not get
involved in a prairie Frisbee
throwing contest soon after a
rainstorm.

A Real Texan stays clear of
nudist camps where they can't
tell if he's a Real Texan.

WORK

A Real Texan can fix anything from a bulldozer to a hairdryer with baling wire, chewing gum, and duct tape.

If you see riders working cattle wearing gimme caps, they are probably Real Texas cowboys. Drugstore cowboys now wear the fanciest hats.

A Real Texan won't like it if you insinuate he wears a big belt buckle to make an impression on his cows.

Real Texans always climb over a barbed wire fence, never crawl under it. The barbs on top are nothing to what you might bump into on the ground.

A Real Texan doesn't put a pinch of wintergreen or peppermint-flavored snuff between his cheek and gums. He chomps off a big chew of thick plug Tensley.

A Real Texan feels great sympathy for a Brahma bull in a cactus patch.

A Real Texan might not have an oilwell, but he usually has five or six in the talking stage.

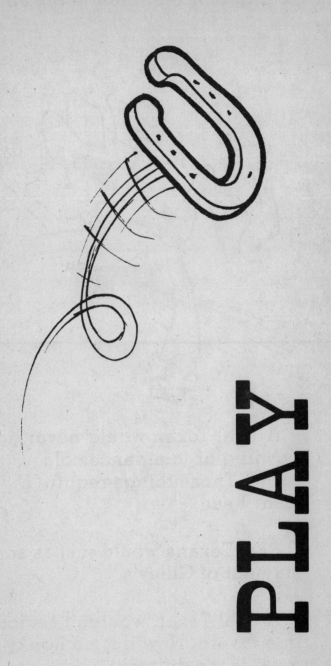

PLAY

A Real Texan would rather go
to a tractor pull than to the circus.

A Real Texan would never go
bowling or to a dance cold
sober. Those things require a
clear head.

Real Texans would just as soon
stay out of Gilley's.

A Real Texan wouldn't set foot
in a tavern. Now if it's a honky
tonk, that's different.

To the Real Texan, the only
real dance tune is *Cotton-Eyed
Joe*. It's the only song he can
remember the lyrics to.

A Real Texan uses his pocket
knife to clean his fingernails, turn
the barbecue, clean his boot heels,
perform minor surgery, and
cut the cheese at parties. He's
no Texan if he ever washes the blade.

Real Texans don't play golf.
They pitch horseshoes,
preferably when the horse is not
wearing them.

A Real Texan, if he's a
gentleman, remembers to take off
his spurs before he goes to bed.

TALK

A Real Texan never says "REAALLY."

A Real Texan doesn't say "You-all." He says "Y'all."

A Real Texan never begins a sentence with "Hopefully . . . ," he does not refer to "the mass media," and he doesn't know what's "viable" or care what "the bottom line" is. He does say "I seen" and "I done."

A Real Texan believes a faggot is a piece of firewood.

A Real Texan will often refer to mountain oysters by their generic name.

Real Texans know how to pronounce FAJITAS.

Real Texans are bilingual
when they are trying to negotiate
a date.

Real Texans crack PE-CONS
and think PE-CANS are
something that goes under the
bed and empties out a window.

A Real Texan is likely to fly off the handle when he hears RODEO pronounced ro-DAY-o.

A Real Texan knows how to spell Waxahachie.

A Real Texan can spit between his front teeth and hiss obscenities beginning with the letter S at the same time.

Real Texans do not say
BARBED WIRE. The correct
pronunciation is BOB WAR.

A Real Texan never calls
anybody a son-of-a-bitch. The
word is SOMBITCH.

It isn't nice to call a Real
Texan a sombitch — or safe,
either.

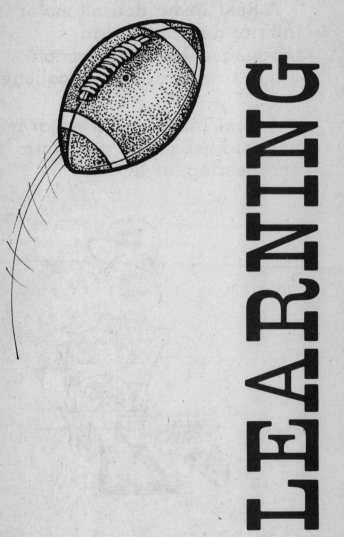

LEARNING

A Real Texan believes in bilingual education so long as he doesn't have to study English.

A Real Texan doesn't major in interior design, foreign languages, Radio-Television-Films, or psychology in college.

A Real Texan might major in animal husbandry, petroleum engineering, or ROTC.

ANIMAL HUSBANDRY 101

No Real Texan's education is complete unless he has memorized *Texas History Movies*.

A Real Texan doesn't understand why a big, fast football player has to make good grades.

As soon as a Real Texan learns to count, he learns how to play 42.

CULTURE

Real Texans don't give a snap for armadillos on a T-shirt or in a pot.

It isn't art to a Real Texan unless it has horns, antlers, gills, hooves, or feathers.

A Real Texan would never use breath mints or insect repellant.

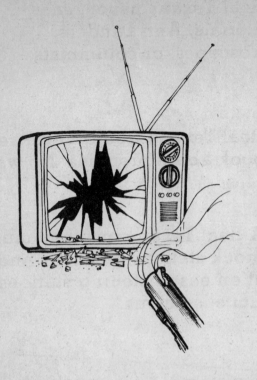

A Real Texan never watches the television show *Dallas*. Yet he sort of hopes someone really will shoot J.R.

Real Texans do not read the *New Republic, Texas Monthly,* Doonesbury, or the *Houston Chronicle*. They DO read *Texas Football, Field and Stream, Sports Illustrated,* Tank McNamara, and the *Dallas Cowboy Weekly*.

Real Texans never read
editorials, Ann Landers,
horoscopes, or columnists.

Real Texans would never read
a book about preppies. No way.

A Real Texan considers music
on rock stations seditious and
that on easy-listening stations
"dam suspicious."

A Real Texan would not know
that Van Cliburn is a Texan. In
fact, Real Texans would not
know what a Van Cliburn is.

The Real Texan has never seen
a Fellini movie (sounds dirty). He
has seen *The Good, the Bad and
the Ugly* twice and *Hang 'em
High* three times. He wishes they
would bring back John Wayne to
make some real motion pictures
again.

A Real Texan never scratches his crotch in public unless something itches.

A Real Texan doesn't need an analyst because he's so simple a psychiatrist would never figure him out.

SPORTS

A Real Texan knows baseball is NOT America's Favorite Pastime.

A Real Texan could never confuse the Astrodome with the Coonastrodome in New Orleans.

A Real Texan would never have fired Bum Phillips.

Real Texan definition of a turncoat: A Texas blue chip football player who signs with "The University of Texas at Norman."

Darryl Royal is not a Real Texan. He is an Okie and must suffer for the sin of his father for settling there.

Real Texans root for the Oklahoma Sooners only when the Sooners are playing Notre Dame.

A Real Texan knows Tom Landry is not picking his nose on national television. He is signaling a play from the sidelines.

Texas A&M graduates like to refer to the University of Texas football team as the Steers. The University of Texas graduates prefer to concentrate on the Horns.

WOMEN

Real Texans believe in the double standard, so long as it doesn't apply to women.

A Real Texas Woman believes in the double standard, too — until she catches him.

A Real Texan does not like a woman who is smarter than he, which could make him an endangered species.

A Real Texan won't marry until his intended has read *Thirteen Days to Glory*.

The Real Texan believes in equal rights for women, so long as they know their place.

A Real Texas Woman knows her place — on the 50-yard-line at the Cotton Bowl.

A Real Texan believes it is not gentlemanly to use profanity around womenfolk, unless they know more cuss words than he does.

A Real Texas honeymoon is a tour of the Buckhorn Saloon.

A Real Texan never lets his wife take out the garbage. That is a chore for the children.

A Real Texan gives his wife guns and dogs for birthdays and anniversaries. A Real Texas Woman doesn't mind. That's what she would have asked for, anyway.

A Real Texan goes rattlesnake hunting to get away from his wife and drink longnecks with the boys. When he goes deer hunting, she goes along.

A Real Texas Woman does not expose hairy underarms to public view.

A Real Texas Woman can baste a mean brisket or host a tea for the Court of St. James. Ask Anne Armstrong.

A Real Texas Woman never goes into the water wearing her bikini and cowgirl boots.

A Real Texas Woman never wears her spurs to bed, either.

OTHER STATES

A Real Texan would rather stay at the Menger Hotel than the Greenbriar.

A Real Texan never wears his hat in the house or in a cafe. Those people are from Arkansas.

A Real Texan believes Alaska is still the largest U.S. territory.

Real Texans don't go to Colorado to cool off in the summer. They stay home and suffer like men.

Real Texans never, never go to Oklahoma — unless, of course, the law is right behind them.

A Real Texan knows there is a Yankee in the house when someone orders catsup and relish on his hamburger.

Real Texans don't eat charcoal, so they never order their steaks well-done. Real Texans don't order rice with their hamburgers. Those people are from Louisiana.

A Real Texan believes any steak that is bad enough to require steak sauce to give it flavor probably came from Argentina. It is said even the hamburger meat from the Argentine is tough.

Real Texans think Anita Bryant is a little strange. How else could she prefer Florida orange juice over that of Texas?

Real Texans weren't joking when they said, "Let them (Yankees) freeze to death in the dark."

Las Vegas is about as close to California as a Real Texan cares to go.

A Real Texan could tell the California governor how to get rid of the Medfly. Texans sterilized their male flies and sent them out to mate so they produced no screwworms. How could a Texan explain that to a Californian?

TEXAS

A Real Texan will give you directions to anywhere in the state, even if he doesn't know where it's at.

Real Texans think Willie Nelson ought to be president.

A Real Texan thinks San Jacinto Day should be a national holiday and that Texas would be better off still a Republic. He will fight to the death to keep it from being cut up into five new states.

A Real Texan never tells Polish, ethnic, or Little Moron jokes. He tells Aggie jokes.

Real Texans recognize two plots of hallowed ground — the Alamo and the artificial turf of Texas Stadium.

Real Texans believe a historical marker should be installed at La Grange in honor of a real Chicken Ranch.

Real Texans don't have to go to any other state to watch lurid, sexy murder trials involving the filthy rich.

A Real Texan knows that "The Eyes of Texas" is not the state song.

Despite what a Real Texan might tell you, a hunting license is not required to kill a Texas cockroach.

No matter where he is, a Real Texan acts like he owns the place. A lot of the time he does.

Real Texans don't worry about being Real Texans because they never thought about it before.